Techn
Changes Our
World

Printed in Mexico

ISBN-13: 978-0-15-367357-3
ISBN-10: 0-15-367357-5

3 4 5 6 7 8 9 10   050   13 12 11 10 09 08

Harcourt
SCHOOL PUBLISHERS

Visit *The Learning Site!* www.harcourtschool.com

Bringing People Together

When people communicate, they share ideas and information. In the past, it was hard for people to communicate. If a friend moved to another state, sending a letter could take weeks or months. If the friend moved to another country, it could take even longer!

The post office used to deliver mail by horse and wagon. In 1822, a letter took 11 days to go from Washington, D.C., to Nashville, Tennessee. Today, it may only take a day or two.

Today, machines help sort the mail. Years ago, people had to do this work by hand.

Today, e-mail is the fastest mail of all. Your notes can go around the world in minutes.

In the early 1970s, e-mail was a new idea. Only a few people knew about it. Even fewer used it. Now millions of people around the world use e-mail to communicate every day.

Today, people use computers for fun, school, and work. E-mail is so fast that many people call regular mail "snail mail." They think that compared to e-mail, regular mail moves as slow as a snail. Thanks to e-mail, people all over the world can communicate faster than ever.

Armchair Travel

Today, people can "visit" other places without leaving home. People use the Internet to look at pictures of faraway places. They read to find out more about those places. The Internet makes the world seem smaller.

One way to learn about a place is by taking a virtual tour. A virtual tour makes the person who is watching feel as if he or she is really there. It can show pictures and movies while telling a story.

The Internet makes learning about faraway places fun.

Webcams

The Internet helps people learn about important places in the world. Many of these places have webcams. Webcams are video cameras. People can watch on the Internet what the cameras record.

Some IMAX theaters surround viewers.

IMAX movies are a fun way to learn, too. IMAX cameras use the largest film in the world. The movies are shown on big screens. Some IMAX screens are so big that they cover the ceiling and the walls around the seats!

Mapping Places

In the past, people used maps and globes to look at places. They help people learn where places are located and how to get there. Today, there are new ways to find this information.

Many websites show maps. People can type in an address and a map of that place will appear. These maps can be changed to show a large or a small area. They can show a street, a city, a country, or even the world. Some websites give directions.

Some cars have small computers that give directions.

People can use satellite photographs to make many kinds of maps.

Pictures taken from space are called satellite photographs. A satellite is something that circles something else in space. Many satellites circle Earth and take pictures.

Satellite photographs show things that maps do not. They show how things look in real life. Some photographs are so clear that swimming pools, cars, and people can be seen. Some people can find satellite photographs of their street on the Internet.

News Around the World

Getting news is important to people all over the world. In the past, most people got news by newspaper. This was slow. People had to wait for newspapers to print the news. Today, people can get news fast.

Radio, television, and the Internet are all ways to get news fast. They tell news as it happens. They share news from all over the world.

Today it is easy to keep track of news from around the world.

Some people use computers to tell the weather.

Cameras are used to show people the news. Some cameras are used to take pictures as news happens. Others take videos. Cameras bring the news to people. They make people feel as if they are where the news happens.

Satellites also help share news. Some satellites were made to tell the weather. They can warn people of bad storms. This helps save lives. Other satellites carry information. They help news travel fast.

24-Hour News

TV news changed in 1980. A new station called CNN, or Cable News Network was started. CNN showed news 24 hours a day. This idea was new. Many people did not think it was a good idea. But today people depend on CNN for news 24-hours a day.

Learning New Customs

Learning about customs in different countries is easier than ever. Many big companies have offices all over the world. Some workers move from one country to another. People share their customs. One custom they love to share is food.

Many restaurants serve food from other countries. People can taste food from other places. People can buy some of these foods in stores near their homes.

Today, we can eat food from around the world, such as cheese from the Netherlands.

10

Have You Tried Sushi?

People around the world are learning to enjoy sushi. Sushi is a food from Japan. People in Japan have been eating sushi for hundreds of years.

Sushi is made from rice with fish, vegetables, or other foods added. In some restaurants today, a machine keeps plates of sushi rolling by.

Fresh food used to be difficult to ship. Now, special freezers and refrigerators keep food fresh. Trucks, trains, and planes can move food from one place to another. People can eat food that was made or grown far away.

Some TV shows teach people how to cook food from around the world. People can use computers or telephones to order food from other countries. They can also find recipes on the Internet.

Today, it is easy to taste many foods from around the world.

Pen Pal Packages

Some people have friends in other countries. They write e-mails or letters to each other. These kinds of friends are called pen pals. Some school classes are pen pals to classes in other countries. They write to each other to learn how they are alike and different.

Sometimes people want to send packages to their friends. Today, that is easier and faster than ever. Airplanes, trucks, and ships move mail quickly. A package may only take a day or two to get to another country.

It is fun to send letters and packages to another country.

Planes make mail move fast.

Companies often need to send packages quickly. They may need to get something to someone the next day or even in one hour.

Sometimes when people send packages, they get a special number. They can look up that number on the Internet. It tells where the package is located. It tells people which day their package will arrive.

Today's world moves fast. E-mails can be sent to anyone in the world with an e-mail address. Boxes can be sent quickly, across town or around the world.

Visit Another Country!

Long ago trips took a long time. People had to travel by boat, by horse, or by foot.

Airplanes make travel much faster today. Airplanes are getting bigger and faster. Many carry hundreds of people at one time. People can fly from Florida to Japan in 19 hours or less.

Today, there are airports all over the world. They have become very busy. Flying on a plane is one of the fastest ways to travel.

Today there is plenty to do in big airports. You can shop and eat while you wait.

You can watch a movie or read a book while you fly around the world.

Technology is always changing travel. Today, people can use computers to buy plane tickets. When people fly, they can watch movies and TV. They can listen to music.

Technology is making the world feel smaller. It brings together people from all over the world. It makes it easy for people to communicate.

Busy Airports

Orville and Wilbur Wright made their first flight in 1903, at Kitty Hawk, North Carolina. Now, more than 100 years later, airports are some of the busiest places in the world. About 9.4 million people used the airport in Raleigh, North Carolina, in 2005. That is about 250,000 people each day!

Think and Respond

1. When did people start using e-mail?

2. How do people communicate?

3. How has technology helped spread the news?

4. Why is it easier to try foods from different countries today?

5. Why is travel easier today than it used to be?

 # Activity

Think about the ways people communicate today. Then talk with an adult about what communication was like when they were younger. Make a poster to show old and new ways to communicate. Share the poster with your classmates.